AMISH SHADOWS Light Reflected
A Modern Look at a Traditional Design

Our journey writing this book began many years ago with the block Kathryn's grandmother called Sunshine and Shadows. It wasn't until years later that she learned the block was also known as Roman Stripes, and is much more widely known as Amish Shadows. In the late 19th century Amish women began to sell their quilts as a way of supplementing their family income. Amish quilts are traditionally hand-sewn and hand-quilted. They use bright colors with black backgrounds and are visually striking. Antique Amish quilts are highly prized. Modern Amish quilts are also works of art. This block began to be used by Amish quilters early in the 20th century and has remained a favorite because it lends itself so well to the Amish color scheme and simplicity of design.

Amish Shadows has become one of our favorite blocks because while simple, it has great design potential. New ideas continue to come to us. We encourage all of you to play with the block and create some new settings of your own.

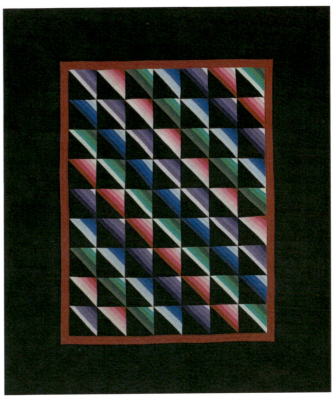

Amish Shadows Quilt from Upstate New York

Part way through the design process Kathryn talked to Lynn about testing one of her patterns. They collaborated on several other quilt tops and much more. Lynn also spearheaded two testing days with the quilters who assisted by trying our patterns and making many of the quilts pictured in this book.

The pattern testers were: Mary McNamara, Lynn Lauzon-Russom, Mary Ellen Tardiff, Noel Payton, Deb Kreifels, Lee Poremba, Bromwyn Helene, and Carolyn Dollard. Tom and Eileen McCabe and Kathie Lutz edited the patterns, making many good suggestions. Barb and Steve Rothe opened their home for photos of the quilts in their "natural habitat." In addition, our families have been supportive and encouraging throughout the writing and publishing process. Our gratitude and thanks go to all of these wonderful people.

Now a new book is beginning to take form in our collaborative brains — watch for **Roads to Everywhere, Ladders to Heaven** coming soon.

Happy Quilting and Peace,

Kathryn R Greenwold   *Lynn Reynolds Malecki*

AMISH SHADOWS Light Reflected

I began quilting with my grandmothers in Nebraska. At age 6 I sat under the quilt in my grandmother's front parlor and threaded needles for the ladies who came once a week to quilt for church mission work. By age 10 I was hand-sewing my own blocks. From these simple lessons during summer vacations a life-long passion was born. Because I was first exposed to quilting at its most traditional, I wanted to learn where these "rules" of quilting came from. It was during this study that I discovered Amish quilts, and a new passion was born.

When we moved to upstate New York I had a hard time finding rewarding work that still allowed me to be home when my children were home. What began as a hobby grew into my vocation. I now teach in shops and for guilds, lecture to community groups, travel to teach and judge quilt shows, and design patterns. This book was the next logical step in my professional development. My husband, Larry, and I have four grown children and two grandchildren. Family and friends, especially my friend Lauretta who is not a quilter, but who is my greatest cheerleader, are the other main focus of my life.

Peace,

Kathryn

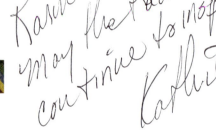

Karin — May the traditional continue to inspire! Kathie

I began sewing in 4-H under my mother's instruction making everything from aprons to prom gowns. The fascination with the quilt arts came to me in a blizzard, when the school where I was teaching music education in Hoboken, New Jersey was closed for an entire week. With scraps of fabric, an old sewing machine and limitless possibilities, the quilt bug stung through all three layers; my heart, mind and soul.

Since then, I have enjoyed learning from master quilters, trying various new techniques, and teaching at the local quilt shop. Working in collaboration with other quilters has broadened my passion for the art form. I enjoy exploring the shared skills and artistry between teaching choral music and teaching quilting.

My husband Keith, family and friends have been very supportive of my work. Our young daughter Katherine has learned how to quilt already with her Grammy and me. Meanwhile, her little brother, Ryan, loves to press the reverse button on the sewing machine while she works on her quilts. It is with deep appreciation and gratitude for Kathryn Greenwold's inspiration and vision that I participate in this first book from KayLynn Designs.

Peace,

Lynn

Contents

Quilts shown here from top to bottom are Italian Tile pieced by Lynn Reynolds Makrin and long-arm machine quilted by Eileen McCabe; Spring in the Catskills, a variation of Catskill Mountainscape pieced and home machine quilted by Kathryn Greenwold; Times Square pieced by Lynn and quilted by Mandy Leins with a Traditional Throw in the background pieced and quilted by Kathryn; and Sunshine Star pieced and hand quilted with both big stitch and standard stitch by Kathryn.

Basic Sewing Instructions

*Once mastered, the simple steps below will provide what is needed to create any of the quilts included in this book. Please read through both the **Basic Sewing Instructions** and the specific instructions for your **Project** before starting your quilt.*

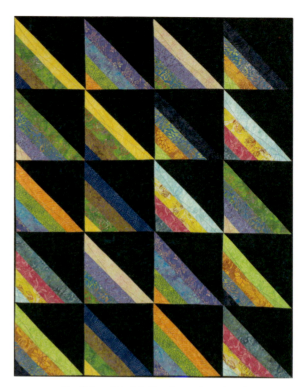

Traditional Amish Shadows pieced and home machine quilted by Kathryn Greenwold

The Design Block

The main building block for all of the quilts in this book is the Amish Shadows **Design Block**. By using it in different orientations and combinations, you can create many different designs.

Figure 1
Design Block

The **Design Block** includes a half-square triangle made up of *4 fabric strips (S1 – S4)* of equal widths ( ) and a *half-square triangle* ( ) of a contrasting background fabric. Traditionally, this block was made with brightly colored strips on one side and black fabric as the background.

The Amish use only solid colors. However, the quilts included in this book are not all traditional. We have used print fabrics, solids, batiks, light backgrounds, hand dyes, and other variations to illustrate the possibilities that can be created with this basic block. In the graphic diagrams found throughout the book, our **Background** fabric will be red and the **Design Units** will be shades of aqua. Please refer to the photographs of quilts throughout this book and use your imagination in choosing your own color combinations.

Choosing Fabric

Yardage requirements for each project are found in the **Project** instructions. For each **Project**, you need a strip pack **or** 4 fabrics **(S1-S4)** for your strips along with a background fabric. The strips should range from light to dark (S1 being the lightest and S4 the darkest). Some **Projects** include additional background squares and rectangles, and borders. You will also need backing, binding, and batting. Yardage requirements given are generous estimates.

If using a strip pack, separate your fabrics into sets of light, medium-light, medium-dark, and dark before doing any sewing to make sure you have equal amounts of each value.

> **NOTE:** The most important factors in choosing fabrics are the **visual value** (light to dark/bright to somber relationship) of the strip-pieced fabrics and the **contrast** with your background. These differences can be very subtle for a soft look or extreme for a vibrant look. The 4 strips in each strip set should, however, range in value from light to dark with a medium-light and medium-dark value fabric for the two center strips. If you have difficulty discerning these differences, use a **value viewer** to help place your fabrics.

There are examples of these color/value differences in the quilts pictured throughout the book. Here are a few groups of fabrics that would work well:

Solid strip pack with black background for an Amish look — note the variety of color and visual value.

Blue batiks with a dark background.

Autumnal prints with a light print background.

Civil War Reproductions with a light background to the far left and a dark background to the far right. Note S1 is lighter than the light background option.

Most fabric cuts will be made across the **width of the fabric (WOF)** to give you the strip length. You will be strip piecing or cutting other units from these strips. The width of strips used will vary from project to project. The **Cutting Instructions** for your **Project** will provide specific information. If you precut everything, use plastic zip-top bags to store precut units before using them. This will be especially helpful in keeping track of units that are similar in size but used for different areas of the quilt.

Yardage for borders is based on WOF cuts. If you do not want to piece your borders additional yardage may be needed.

> **NOTE:** You may want to cut your fabric in stages, as you need it. For example, cut just the strips and make the strip sets. Then cut the background fabric when you are ready to make the blocks. This will allow you to make adjustments if your sewing varies from the expected strip set size.

Quilt-As-You-Go

Most of the **Projects** in this book are assembled in rows or large units. They could easily be adapted to quilt-as-you-go projects. Additional backing may be needed to allow the extra fabric to join the rows and/or units.

Basic Equipment Needed

Sewing machine

Machine and hand sewing kit — pins, scissors, marking tool, etc.

Rotary cutter, mat, 24" × 6" ruler and 6 ½", 8 ½" or 12 ½" square (depending on the **Design Block** size for your **Project**)

Thread for both piecing and quilting

Spray sizing — optional

Zip-top plastic bags to store precut units — optional

Creating the Design Blocks

Creating the strip sets for Design Units:

1. Either cut **1 strip** from each of your **4 fabrics (S1-S4)** to the strip width designated in the **Project** instructions by the WOF *OR* select **4 strips** (ranging from light to dark) from a strip pack.

2. Line up the strips from lightest to darkest **(S1, S2, S3, S4)**.

3. Sew the two lighter fabrics together lengthwise **(S1 and S2)**.

4. Sew the two darker fabrics together lengthwise **(S3 and S4)**.

5. Sew these two units together, joining the medium dark **(S3)** to the medium light **(S2)** strip. Sew this seam in the opposite direction from the two steps above to avoid distortion in your strip sets (Figure 2).

6. Set the seams by pressing the seam allowance flat, before opening them (Figure 3).

Figure 2

7. Press the seams to the darker fabric (Figure 4). To avoid distorting the strip set, don't use steam — instead try a little spray sizing.

8. Finally, press firmly from the right side of the strip set to eliminate any "pleating" or distortion of the seams (Figure 5).

Figure 3

Figure 4

Figure 5

> **NOTE:** Your strips may be slightly different in length. It won't matter in cutting your half-squares as long as they are approximately the same length.

Each strip set should be consistent in width. See the chart below.

Width of Strips Used	Width of 4 Strips Sewn Together (Strip Set) 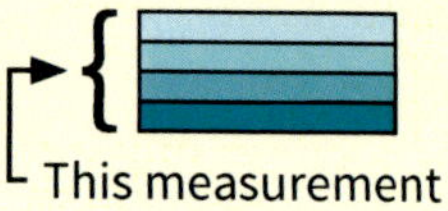 ⌐{ This measurement	Size of Background Unit Squares Before Cutting 	Unfinished Size of Assembled Design Block 
1" × WOF	2 ½" × WOF	3 ½" × 3 ½"	2 ¾" × 2 ¾"
1 ¼" × WOF	3 ½" × WOF	5" × 5"	4 ¼" × 4 ¼"
1 ½" × WOF	4 ½" × WOF	6 ½" × 6 ½"	6" × 6"
2" × WOF	6 ½" × WOF	9 ¼" × 9 ¼"	8 ⅜" × 8 ⅜"
2 ½" × WOF	8 ½" × WOF	12" × 12"	11 ½" × 11 ½"

Chart 1

If your strip sets do not match these ideal measurements, you have two choices:

1. Correct your seam allowances to be exact.

OR

2. If all your strip sets are consistently larger or smaller than the ideal measurement, adjust the size when cutting your **Background Units**. Trim all the completed **Design Blocks** to the same new size. Dimensions of your quilt may be altered slightly. Check yardage needs for your background, border, and backing fabrics.

> **NOTE:** Cutting with precision, sewing a consistent ¼" seam and pressing carefully are important to the accuracy of your blocks. Measurements for **Background Units** were rounded up. Trim down as needed after completing the **Design Blocks**.

Cutting the strip-pieced half-squares (Design Units):

You will get a different number of half-squares (**Design Units**) from your strip sets depending on the width of the strip set (see Chart 2). The **Project** Instructions will tell you the total number of **Design Units** you need to complete your quilt top.

Strip Width	Strip Set Width	Design Units Cut from Each Set
1" strips	2 ½"	10
1 ¼" strips	3 ½"	9
1 ½" strips	4 ½"	8
2" strips	6 ½"	6
2 ½" strips	8 ½"	4

Chart 2

> **NOTE:** Half of your **Design Units** will be light-tipped and half will be dark-tipped (Figure 6). While most of the **Projects** will use both in your quilt top, some use more of one than the other or perhaps only one type of **Design Unit** — light- or dark-tipped.
>
> If the **Project** you are working on uses only light- or only dark-tipped **Design Units**, begin cutting your strips with that type of unit. This will maximize the number of light- or dark-tipped half-squares you will get from each strip set. Save the unused **Design Units** for another **Project**.

Cutting Instructions

Cut 45° triangles from the strip set, referring to Figure 6 below. Use a square ruler large enough to allow you to make the cuts without shifting the ruler (Figures 7 and 8).

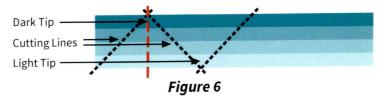

Figure 6

Figure 7

Figure 8

1. Starting from the left if left-handed and from the right if right-handed, cut the first triangle with the wide part of the triangle at the base (Figure 7). You may be able to use the cut edge as is; however it is good to check that it is still accurate as the triangle may get a little "tilted" as you move down the strip.

2. For the next triangle, either shift the ruler up so the point is down (Figure 8), or rotate your cutting board so that the opposite side of the strip set is close to you. Cut the second triangle.

3. Continue down the strip in this fashion until you have cut as many triangles as possible.

Save the leftover partial strips and half-unit sections to use in a scrappy project, for your borders, or on the back of your quilt.

NOTE: The wider your strip set, the more difficult it will be to cut your half-squares accurately. Take care, using good cutting techniques. Let the markings on the ruler help you.

- Measure the length of each side of your triangles.
- Use the diagonal line on the ruler — check that it is vertical to the strips.
- Check that the horizontal seam lines of the strips cross the squares on the ruler at the same place all the way across.

If you do not have a square ruler, you may use the 45° line on a 24" × 6" ruler to line up your cuts. However, you will find your cuts easier to make and more accurate using a square.

Cutting the Background Units:

You will need one half-square triangle of background fabric (**Background Unit**) for each **Design Unit** to complete the **Design Blocks**. The **Project** instructions will list the sizes and number of squares to cut. Complete your **Background Units** using the instructions below.

1. Cut the background fabric into strips using the size indicated in the **Project** instructions.
2. Subcut each strip into squares as directed.
3. Cut each square into 2 half-square triangles. ◨

Figure 9

Complete the Design Blocks:

1. Assemble the blocks by sewing one **Background Unit** to one of the **Design Units** along the diagonal edge, using a ¼" seam. Press the seam to the background fabric.

   Chain piece (Figure 9) your blocks to save both time and thread. Trim the "wings" (Figure 10) from your triangles once the blocks are assembled and pressed.

2. Once you have sewn all the required **Design Blocks**, measure them to ensure they are a uniform size. If they are not, check that the seams are pressed flat. Finally, sliver trim the blocks to a uniform square size as needed.

Figure 10

Assembling the Quilt

If your **Project** calls for additional background squares and rectangles, follow the **Cutting Instructions** for these elements. Several of the **Projects** have **Background Cutting Guides** for the background fabric(s). Cuts may be made vertically for most efficient use of your fabric. Follow the specific **Cutting and Assembly Instructions** for your **Project** to complete your quilt top.

Square Up and Add Borders or Prepare for Quilting

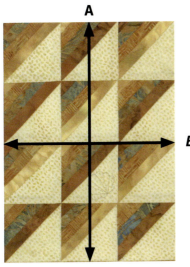

Figure 11

Squaring up your quilt top at this point will help you avoid wavy edges and borders that don't fit. It will also give your quilt greater longevity. Always square your tops, whether you are adding borders or not.

Once your quilt top is complete, lay it out on a design wall, floor, or other flat surface (Figure 11). Measure the length of the quilt at the **center** of the quilt top (**A**). Write down that measurement. Make sure the right and left sides are the same length and trim the top and bottom edges carefully as needed.

Measure the width of the quilt at the **center** (**B**). Write down that measurement. Make sure the top and bottom widths are the same and square up as needed. Once you have added each border, repeat this process and trim as needed.

Add Borders:

If your border is longer than **40" (WOF)**, you need to piece your border strips. You can sew them together along a straight edge or at a 45° angle (see Figures 12 and 13 in the **Binding** section below). You might sew all of the strips cut for each border together to form one long strip. Then cut the lengths you need for each side. Cut these units about 1" longer than the measurement for each side. Adding the top and bottom borders first gives the quilt a more linear feel visually. If the sides are added first the quilt looks wider. You may add the sides first if you would like to. Simply reverse the directions below and measure the quilt top length first. Mitered borders will require additional yardage.

To add borders, use the width measurement you noted above (as determined from the **center** of the quilt) and cut strips and sew the **first border strips on the top and bottom of your quilt**. Press towards the border fabric. Now remeasure the length of the quilt and then cut two strips to about 1" longer than your new measurement. Sew them in place.

For a second border, repeat the process above beginning with new length and width measurements taken from the **center** of the quilt.

Keep in mind that borders do not need to be simple strips of fabric to "finish" the quilt. Experiment with using scraps from your **Project**, using up leftover **Design Blocks**, or completely different blocks.

Backing

If you plan to do your own quilting on a home sewing machine your backing and batting need to be at least 4" larger than the top. Your backing and batting need to be 6-8" larger than the top if quilting on a long-arm machine.

For any quilt more than 74" in both directions a wide backing fabric — usually 106" or 108" wide could be considered. For a 74" width or length you will need 82" of backing to accommodate a long-arm quilting machine, which might not be achieved with two lengths of standard width fabric once the selvages have been trimmed. Anything 80" in length or width would require 3 widths of standard fabric. Wider backing fabric will be both easier to work with and possibly less expensive. What is leftover could be used for your binding.

Remove the selvages from your fabric, sew lengthwise ½" seams, and iron the entire backing thoroughly. Press all seams to one side for strength.

> **NOTE:** A suggestion from a professional long-arm quilter is to cut your last border ½" to 1" wider than needed. This allows for shrinkage during quilting and gives you or your professional the ability to trim straight and square while maintaining the desired border size.

Quilting Your Top

An Amish Shadows quilt would traditionally have been hand quilted either in-the-ditch or with a ¼" outline within the pieced areas. A small floral or feathered pattern would be stitched in the solid half of each block. Feathered vines or cables would then be quilted in the border areas. See drawings here.

Thread color is a consideration because you will be quilting through both very light and very dark areas. Variegated thread might work well overall. If you are recreating an Amish-style quilt, use dark (or light) thread matching your background color, even if machine quilting.

The quilts pictured throughout this book provide examples of many types of quilting. Do what you are comfortable with and what will enhance the visual impact of your quilt.

Depending on the layout for your **Project**, there will be different background areas which will lend themselves to more complex quilting patterns. You might consider doing some big-stitch hand quilting, and then finish your quilt on the machine. Experiment a little and see what works. Once your quilting is completed, trim and square up all three layers of the quilt so the edges are straight and the corners are square, like you did when squaring your quilt top. (See the section "Square Up and Add Borders" on the previous page.)

Binding

After quilting your **Project**, you need to bind it. 2" or 2 ¼" strips are recommended for your binding, even though a slightly wider strip is standard. 2 ¼" will turn well and line up evenly on the front and back of your quilt which is something judges look for.

To determine binding requirements, measure all four sides of the quilt and add them together. Add about 12" to allow for mitered corners. Divide this number by 40 (WOF) which will give you the number of strips you need to cut. Multiply the result by 2 or 2.25 (depending on the width of your strips) to determine the yardage required. For example, if all four sides of a quilt add up to 230", the calculation would be as follows: 230 ÷ 40 = 5.75. The fraction (.75) means you will need 6 binding strips. 6 × 2.25 = 13.5" yardage required. This is exactly ⅜ yard. A ½ yard gives you some extra.

With right sides together join the strips using a 45° seam. Trim the seam to ¼" and press it open to make one continuous strip. Refer to Figures 12 and 13. Trim the "wings" after pressing.

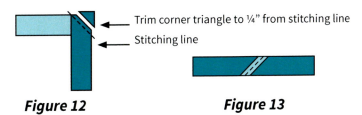

Figure 12   **Figure 13**

Fold in half lengthwise with wrong sides together and press. Apply the strip to your quilt, beginning near the center of one side and using your walking foot. Line up the raw edges of the binding and quilt. Stitch a ¼" seam to attach your binding, leaving about 4" unsewn as you begin (Figure 14). Stop ¼" before the first corner, backstitch, and cut the threads. Fold the binding and begin sewing again as shown in Figures 15 and 16 below.

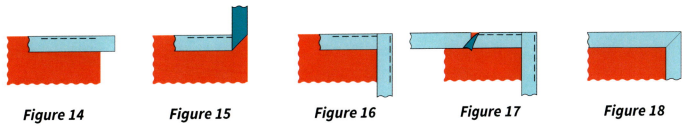

Figure 14   **Figure 15**   **Figure 16**   **Figure 17**   **Figure 18**

Continue stitching and turning corners in the same manner. When you are within a few inches of the beginning, stop stitching leaving your needle in the quilt. Trim the binding to about 1 ½" longer than what is needed to complete the binding.

Fold the beginning edge back about ½" and insert the end of binding into this fold. Complete sewing the binding in place. Refer to Figure 17. Hand or machine turn the binding to the back of the quilt and sew in place. Miter the corners and tack in place. See Figure 18.

For a bias binding, follow the instructions here:

Cut square in half on one diagonal.

Sew the two halves with right sides together using a ¼" seam allowance.

Press seam open.

Draw lines on the wrong side of fabric, spaced the cut width of binding.

Bring diagonal edges together to form a tube with lines offset by one width. Join the diagonal edges with a ¼" seam allowance; press seam open.

Cut along drawn lines to form a continuous bias binding strip.

This method gives you a fully pieced, bias strip that will be easy to attach to your quilt. It takes some practice, but is much quicker and easier than cutting bias strips and joining all of them. Apply your bias binding in the same manner as described above.

Hanging Your Quilt

Check out www.quiltschenectady.org for instructions on how to construct a hanging sleeve. You might also consider purchasing a floor stand or hanging rack for draping your quilt. There are various other instructions and videos on how to make a hanging sleeve available online.

Variations

You may enlarge or reduce the size of a given **Project** by using a wider or narrower strip. Calculate the new size for each quilt using Chart 3 below. Yardage requirements would have to be recalculated for any change in a **Project** design. We leave it to you to make these calculations. When changing the size of a **Project**, take the borders into consideration as well. They should be proportional to the new size of the quilt. For example, a miniature quilt would be overwhelmed by a 4" border, but a Queen or King size quilt might need a 6" border, or several borders. If uncertain about the size border you should use, look at **Projects** in this book that are made in the size you are considering and have confidence in what looks good to you.

Multiply the number of blocks you plan to make for each row by the finished size of the block to calculate the width of your quilt. Multiply the planned number of rows by the finished size of the block to calculate the length of your quilt. For example, a quilt using 1 ½" strips set with 5 blocks in 6 rows would be calculated as follows: 5 × 5.5" = 27.5" wide and 6 × 5.5" = 33" long without borders.

Strip Size	Unfinished Size of Design Blocks	Finished Size of Design Blocks
1" × WOF	2 ¾" × 2 ¾"	2 ¼" × 2 ¼"
1 ¼" × WOF	4 ¼" × 4 ¼"	3 ¾" × 3 ¾"
1 ½" × WOF	6" × 6"	5 ½" × 5 ½"
2" × WOF	8 ⅜" × 8 ⅜"	8" × 8" **
2 ½" × WOF	11 ½" × 11 ½"	11" × 11"

Chart 3

** The actual size would be 7 ⅞" × 7 ⅞" but when estimating the size of a redesigned quilt, using 8" × 8" will be much easier.

As you perfect your technique for creating the Amish Shadows Design Block, play with graph paper or an electronic quilt design program and create your own patterns. For inspiration, take a look at the Gallery pages (inside back and back cover) which includes Projects from the book, textile art, a pastoral stole, and other variations of Amish Shadows.

Traditional Amish Shadows
Three Variations

The Traditional Amish Shadows block is the inspiration for this book. In its simplest form it makes a beautiful quilt. Many variations are possible — both in coloration and in size. Experiment with the block and have fun.

Traditional Amish Shadows Throw pieced and home machine quilted by Bromwyn Helene

Highlights

Highlights	Miniature	Throw	Queen
Skill Level	Beginner	Beginner	Beginner
Strips	1" × WOF (2 sets) 8 strips	2 ½" × WOF (5 sets) 20 strips	2 ½" × WOF (14 sets) 56 strips
Design Units	12	20	56
Background Units	12	20	56
Finished Block Size	2 ¾" × 2 ¾"	11 ½" × 11 ½"	11 ½" × 11 ½"
Border(s)	1" OR 2" finished	4" finished	1 ½" and 5" finished
Finished Quilt Size	7 ¾" × 10" OR 8 ¾" × 11"	Approx. 52" × 63"	90" × 101"

Materials

Materials	Miniature	Throw	Queen
Strip Size	1"	2 ½"	2 ½"
Blocks	12	20	56
Strip	⅛ yd each from fabrics S1-S4	1 half-pack of 2 ½" strips OR 20 strips 2 ½" × WOF from stash (⅞ yard divided equally between fabrics S1-S4)	2 strip packs (56 strips total) OR 56 strips 2 ½" × WOF from stash (4 ¼ yards total divided equally between fabrics S1-S4)
Background	⅛ yard	1 ½ yard	3 ¾ yards
Border(s)	¼ yd	⅞ yard	⅔ yard for inner border 1 ¼ yards for outer border
Backing	1 fat quarter	3 ½ yards	3 ¼ yards from 108" wide backing OR 9 ¾ yards standard width fabric
Binding	2 — 2" strips	⅔ yards	¾ yard
Batting	12" × 12"	Twin size	King size

Cutting Instructions

The **Traditional Amish Shadows** uses only **Design Blocks** with no additional background units. The following are cutting instructions for the Miniature, Throw and Queen variations.

	Miniature	Throw	Queen
Strips And Sets	2 Strips **1" × WOF** for each fabric **S1-S4** *Make 2 strip sets.*	5 Strips **2 ½" × WOF** for each fabric **S1-S4** *Make 5 strip sets — or use 20 strips from a strip pack.*	14 strips **2 ½" × WOF** for each fabric **S1-S4** *Make 14 strip sets or use 56 strips from 2 strip packs.*
Background	1 Strip **3 ¼" × WOF Subcut** into 6 squares **3½" × 3 ½". Cut** each of these squares into 2 half-square triangles 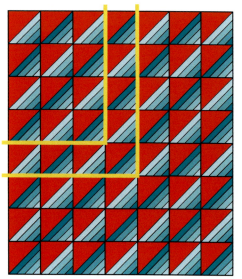 for a total of **12** for the **Design Blocks.**	4 Strips **12" × WOF Subcut** 3 strips into 3 squares **12" × 12".** Cut 1 square **12" × 12"** from the **4th** strip. **Cut** each of these 10 squares into 2 half-square triangles for a total of **20** for the **Design Blocks.**	10 strips **12 × WOF Subcut** 9 strips into 3 squares **12" × 12".** Cut 1 square **12" × 12"** from the **10th** strip. **Cut** each of these **28** squares into 2 half-square triangles for a total of **56** for the **Design Blocks.**
Border(s)	2 Strips **1 ½"** OR **2 ½" × WOF** for the border of your choice	7 strips **4 ½" × WOF**	7 strips **2 ½" × WOF** for inner border and **8 strips 5 ½" × WOF** for outer border.

Block Assembly

Follow the Basic Sewing Instructions for constructing your Design Blocks. Sliver trim all your blocks to a uniform size for ease in assembly.
For the **Miniature** quilt you will need to construct **2 strip sets** for **12 Design Blocks.**
For the **Throw** you will need to construct **5 strip sets** for **20 Design Blocks.**
For the **Queen** size you will need to construct **14 strip sets** for **56 Design Blocks.**

MINIATURE SIZE
7 ¾" × 10" OR 8 ¾" × 11"
1" strips
4 Rows of **3 Design Blocks** each

THROW SIZE
52" × 63"
2 ½" strips
5 Rows of **4 Design Blocks** each

QUEEN SIZE
90" × 101"
2 ½" strips
8 Rows of **7 Design Blocks** each

Quilt Assembly

In laying out your Rows you should alternate the light- and dark-tipped blocks and orient all the blocks facing in the same direction. For all three variations you will alternate the light- and dark-tipped **Design Blocks** in each row, and from row to row. Refer to the graphic on the previous page for visual assistance in sewing your rows together.

Rows A & B — Begin with a dark-tipped block for **Row A**, then begin **Row B** with a light-tipped block.

> For the **Miniature Quilt** make **2** each of **Row A** and **Row B** with **3** blocks in each Row.
>
> For the **Throw** make **3** of **Row A** and **2** of **Row B** with **4** blocks in each Row.
>
> For the **Queen Quilt** make **4** each of **Row A** and **Row B** with **7** blocks in each Row.

> **NOTE:** When sewing your Rows together for any of these variations alternate the direction you press them to reduce distortion of your quilt top. This is especially important in the larger variations. Press the seams between blocks to one side for each **Row A** and to the other side for each **Row B**. This will help in matching and locking the seams while joining the Rows.

Miniature
Join one **Row A** to one **Row B**. Then join the other two Rows. Finally, join the **2** units making sure you sew a **Row B** to a **Row A**.

Throw
Join one **Row A** to one **Row B**. Then join a **Row B** to a **Row A**. Assemble the quilt by joining the first A/B units to the remaining Row A, then add the B/A unit to the bottom of this 3 row unit.

Queen
Join one **Row A** to one **Row B**. Make **4** of these units. Join **2** units making sure you sew a Row B to a Row A. Join the other 2 A/B units. Finally complete the central seam.

Finishing

Refer to the **Basic Sewing Instructions** for some hints on squaring your top, attaching your borders, preparing your backing, sandwiching and quilting your quilt, and preparing and attaching the binding. Consult the **Cutting Instructions** above for the specifics in preparing your border strips.

Variations

If you would like to make **Traditional Amish Shadows** in a different size from these three, you might simply make more blocks in one of the sizes included here. You might also consider using a different size strip for your design blocks. Refer to **Variations** in **Basic Sewing Instructions** to calculate the finished size of this quilt. Yardage requirements must be recalculated for any size variation.

Detail of "Sea, Sand, and Sky," a miniature Traditional Amish Shadows Quilt, with home machine quilting

Field and Fallow

I've always been fascinated by the patterns fields make when viewed from above. Aerial views are the inspiration for this setting. Using only Design Blocks, this quilt is quick to assemble and lends itself to using up your stash.

Highlights

Skill Level:	Beginner
Strips:	**32** strips **2" × WOF** or equivalent yardage
Design Units:	**48** — **24** light-tipped and **24** dark-tipped units
Background Units:	**48** — could be scrappy
Unfinished Block Size:	**8 ⅜" × 8 ⅜"**
Finished Quilt Size:	**48" × 64"**

Pieced by Lynn Reynolds Makrin and long-arm machine quilted by Dianne Podesva

Materials

Strips: **32 strips 2 ½" × WOF from a pre-cut strip pack** cut down to **2" × WOF**

or ⅔ yard each of **4** fabrics — **S1-S4** (light, medium light, medium dark, dark)

or the equivalent in **2" strips** from your stash with a variety of visual values

Background: 1 ¾ yards — could be scrappy

Borders: Field and Fallow as shown here has no borders

Binding: ½ yard

Backing: 3 yards

Batting: Twin

Cutting Instructions

Fabric	First Cut	Subcuts
Strips — 8 each 2" × WOF of fabrics **S1-S4** for **Design Units**.	None	None
Background Units - 48	6 strips, 9 ¼" × WOF	Cut each strip into 4 squares 9 ¼" × 9 ¼". Then cut each square into 2 half-square triangles ◪ for the **Design Blocks**.

Block Assembly

Follow the Basic Sewing Instructions for constructing your Design Blocks. Sliver trim the blocks to a uniform square size. You will need to make 8 strip sets, cutting 6 half-square triangles from each set.

Assemble Field and Fallow in Rows as Follows

 Background Units   Strip Pieced Design Units

Light and dark tipped **Design Blocks** have not been indicated because you may want to place the blocks randomly as was done in the quilt pictured.

 However, for a more systematic placement of the blocks, alternate them throughout the rows in this way.

> **NOTE:** Make **2** of each of the rows pictured below. Pay attention to the orientation of each **Design Block** as you assemble your rows.

Rows A & E

Rows B & F

Press all the seams between blocks to one side. Alternate the direction pressed row to row to aid in matching the seams between the rows.

Join **Rows A & B**. Join **Rows E & F**.

> **NOTE:** Carefully match and lock the seams between **Design Blocks** while joining your rows. Press the seams between rows open to reduce bulk.

Rows C & G

Rows D & H

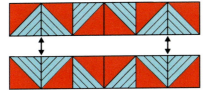

Join **Rows C & D** and **G & H**.

Assemble two 4-row units by joining the **A/B** and **C/D** units and the **E/F** and **G/H** units, again paying attention to the orientation of the blocks. Sew these two 4-row units together to complete your top. Refer to the photograph on the opposite page for additional guidance in setting your rows.

Finishing

Refer to the **Basic Sewing Instructions** for some hints on squaring your top, preparing your backing, sandwiching and quilting your quilt, and preparing and attaching the binding.

Variations

If you would like to make **Field and Fallow** in a different size, consider using a different size strip for your **Design Blocks**. Refer to **Variations** in **Basic Sewing Instructions** to calculate the finished size of this quilt. Yardage requirements must be recalculated for any of these variations. You might also make more blocks and/or add a border or two. Additional yardage would be required.

Detail of Field and Fallow with long-arm quilting

Barn Raising

Barn Raising is a traditional setting. It is one of my favorite ways to set either Amish Shadows or Log Cabin blocks. The quilt pictured here is made using print fabrics and only the light-tipped Design Blocks. However, a larger Barn Raising quilt could be made with light- and dark-tipped blocks, alternating round to round.

Barn Raising pieced and home machine quilted by Kathryn Greenwold

Highlights

Skill Level:	Beginner
Strips:	**2"** strips — **6** sets
Design Units:	**16** light-tipped half-square triangles
Background Units:	**16** half-square triangles
Unfinished Block Size:	Approximately **8 ⅜" × 8 ⅜"**
Finished Quilt Size:	**38" × 38"**

Materials

Strips:	½ yard each of **4** fabrics **S1-S4**, light, medium-light, medium-dark, and dark
Background:	¾ yard
Border:	½ yard of the darkest strip fabric **(S4)**
Backing:	2 ¾ yards — this is enough for long-arm machine quilting
Binding:	½ yard — or use what is left after trimming the backing once the quilting is done
Batting:	Crib size

Cutting Instructions

Fabric	Cut	Subcut	Additional Cuts
Strips	**6** strips **2" × WOF** from each fabric **S1-S4**	None	
Background Units	**2** strips **9 ¼" × WOF**	Cut each strip into **8** squares **9 ¼" × 9 ¼"**	Then cut each square into **2** half-square triangles ◩ for a total of **16** half-squares.
Border	**4** strips **3 ½" × WOF** from fabric **S4**	None — set aside	
Backing	**2** lengths **1 ⅜** yards	None — set aside	

Block Assembly

Follow the Basic Sewing Instructions for constructing your Design Blocks. Sliver trim the blocks to a uniform square size. You will need to make **6** strip sets, cutting **6** half-square triangles from each set. When complete, your **Design Blocks** should measure approximately **8 ⅜" x 8 ⅜"**.

Quilt Assembly

 Background Half-Square   Light-Tipped Design Units

> **NOTE:** All of the **Design Blocks** for **Barn Raising** will have light-tipped strip-pieced units. Save the dark-tipped units for another **Project**, such as **Nautilus**. Pay attention to the orientation of the **Design Blocks** in each row.

Row A
Row B
Row C
Row D

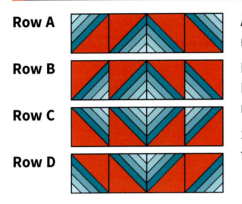

Assemble **Row A** and **Row D**. They are the same, simply oriented to mirror each other. Assemble **Rows B** and **C**.

Press the seams between **Design Blocks** in **Rows A & C** to one side. Press the seams in **Rows B & D** to the opposite side. This will assist in matching and locking the seams when sewing your rows together.

Sew **Rows A & B** together. Sew **Rows C & D** together. Finally, join these two units, paying attention to the orientation of the blocks.

Finishing

Refer to the **Basic Sewing Instructions** for some hints on squaring your top, attaching your borders, preparing your backing, sandwiching and quilting your quilt, and preparing and attaching the binding. Consult the **Cutting Instructions** above for the specifics in preparing your border strips.

Variations

Additional rounds of **Design Blocks** would create a larger quilt. This setting uses **16** blocks. One more round of blocks would create a quilt that is **54" x 54"** (**36** blocks), two rounds would create a double size quilt that is about **70" x 70"** (**64** blocks), and three additional rounds would create a double/queen size quilt that is approximately **86" x 86"** (**100 Design Blocks**). **Additional yardage would be required for all of these enlarged variations.**

If you would like to make **Barn Raising** in a different size, you might also consider using a different size strip for your **Design Blocks**. Refer to **Variations** in **Basic Sewing Instructions** to calculate the finished size of this quilt. Yardage requirements must be recalculated for any of these variations. **Borders should be proportional to your quilt size.**

Detail of Barn Raising with home machine quilting

Sunshine Star

Sunshine Star uses simple placement of the **Design Blocks** to create this large Variable Star pattern. This is another setting reflecting the traditional quilt block while taking on a very modern look.

Highlights

Skill Level:	Beginner
Strips:	8 strips **1 ½" × WOF** — 2 strips of each fabric **S1-S4**
Design Units:	12 — **8** dark-tipped; **4** light-tipped
Background Units:	12
Unfinished Block Size:	**6" × 6"**
Finished Quilt Size:	**28" × 28"**

Pieced and hand quilted by Kathryn Rippeteau Greenwold using hand-dyed fabrics from Dyeing to Sew, Scotia, NY

Materials

Design Units:	¼ yard each of a light, medium-light, medium-dark, and dark fabric **(S1-S4)**
Background Units and Outer Border:	**1** yard of background fabric
First Border:	Cut from fabric **S3**
Backing and Binding:	**1 ½** yards for backing and binding or make your binding from leftovers of the **4** quarter yard cuts **(S1-S4)** and decrease this total by **½** yard

Cutting Instructions

Fabric	First Cut	Subcuts
Strips	2 strips **1 ½" × WOF**	None
Background Units	1 strip **6 ½" × WOF**	6 squares **6 ½" × 6 ½"**. Cut each square into **2** half-square triangles  for a total of 12 half-squares for the **Design Blocks**.
Background Squares	1 strip **6" × WOF**	4 squares **6" × 6"**
Inner Border — Fabric S3	3 strips **1" × WOF**	None
Outer Border — From Background Fabric	3 strips **3 ½" × WOF**	None — set aside for later use

> **NOTE: Sunshine Star** is Fat Quarter friendly for the strip sets (fabrics **S1-S4**). Cut **4** strips from each fabric **1 ½" × 22"** for the **Design Units**. For the inner border, cut **5** strips **1" × 22"** from fabric **S3**.

Block Assembly

Follow the Basic Sewing Instructions for constructing your Design Blocks. Sliver trim the blocks to a uniform square size. You will need to make **2** strip sets, cutting **8** half-square triangles from each set. When complete, your unfinished **Design Blocks** should measure approximately **6" × 6"**.

> **NOTE:** You will have at least **4** light-tipped **Design Units** left over. Save them to use for another **Project**.

Assemble Sunshine Star in Rows as Follows

 Background Units   Dark-Tipped Design Units   Light-Tipped Design Units

> **NOTE:** Pay attention to how the design blocks are oriented as you create the rows.

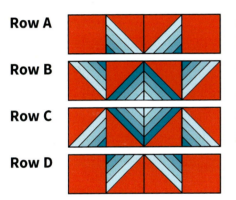

Row A

Row B

Row C

Row D

Assemble **Rows A-D** as shown here. Press the seams to the right in **Rows A & C**.

Press the seams to the left in **Rows B & D**.

Complete your assembly by sewing **Rows A & B** together. Sew **Rows C & D** together. Carefully match and lock the seams between Rows. Then join these two units. Press the seams between Rows open.

Finishing

Refer to the **Basic Sewing Instructions** for some hints on squaring your top, attaching your borders, preparing your backing, sandwiching and quilting your quilt, and preparing and attaching the binding. Consult the **Cutting Instructions** above for the specifics in preparing your border strips.

Variations

To make a larger quilt using the **Sunshine Star** described above you could make multiple units and set them with or without sashing. Four **Sunshine Stars** with a 2" sash and 2 outer borders would measure approximately 62" × 62". Nine **Sunshine Stars** with a 2" sashing and 2 outer borders would measure approximately 90" × 90". Yardage requirements would have to be recalculated.

If you would like to make **Sunshine Star** in a different size, you might consider using a different size strip for your **Design Blocks**. Refer to **Variations** in **Basic Sewing Instructions** to calculate the finished size of this quilt. Yardage requirements must be recalculated for any of these variations.

Detail of Sunshine Star with big stitch and standard hand quilting

Catskill Mountainscape

Inspired by the Ukiyo-e (pictures of the floating world) from ancient Japan, this landscape style ignores the "rules" of perspective, giving the impression that more distant mountains or fields float above whatever is in the foreground. However, it still visually "reads" as a landscape.

Catskill Mountainscape pieced and machine quilted by Mary McNamara

Highlights

Skill Level:	Confident Beginner
Strips:	**1 ¼" × WOF** — **5** sets
Design Units:	**36 total** — **18** light-tipped and **18** dark-tipped units
Background Units:	**18** squares **5" × 5"**
Background Squares:	**4** squares measuring **4 ¼" × 4 ¼"**
Background Rectangles:	**4** rectangles measuring **4 ¼" × 8"**
Unfinished Block Size:	**4 ¼" × 4 ¼"**
Finished Quilt with Borders:	**30 ½" × 38"**

Materials

Strips:	¼ yard of fabrics **S1-S4** (light, medium-light, medium-dark, and dark) *or* **10** strips from a **2 ½"** strip pack **cut in half length-wise**
Background:	**1 ¼** yard
Borders:	**Inner** — ¼ yard, **Outer** — ½ yard
Backing:	**1 ½** yards
Binding:	½ yard
Batting:	Crib size

Cutting Instructions

Fabric	Cut	Subcut	Additional Cuts
Strips	5 strips 1 ¼" × WOF from each fabric S1-S4	None — sort into 5 sets of 4 strips each	None
Background	4 strips 5" × WOF	4 squares 4 ¼" × 4 ¼" 4 rectangles 4 ¼" × 8" 18 squares 5" × 5"	None None Cut these 18 squares in half diagonally ◣ to create **36** half-square triangles for the **Design Blocks**
Inner Border	4 strips 1 ½" × WOF	Set aside	None
Outer Border	5 strips 3 ½" × WOF	Set aside	None

Block Assembly

Follow the Basic Sewing Instructions for constructing your Design Blocks. Sliver trim the blocks to a uniform size. Your first cuts should alternate light-tipped and dark-tipped to get best results from your strip sets.

Assemble Catskill Mountainscape in Rows as Follows

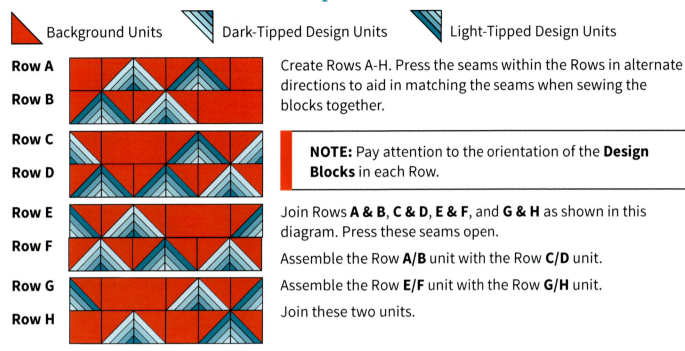

Create Rows A-H. Press the seams within the Rows in alternate directions to aid in matching the seams when sewing the blocks together.

> **NOTE:** Pay attention to the orientation of the **Design Blocks** in each Row.

Join Rows **A & B**, **C & D**, **E & F**, and **G & H** as shown in this diagram. Press these seams open.

Assemble the Row **A/B** unit with the Row **C/D** unit.

Assemble the Row **E/F** unit with the Row **G/H** unit.

Join these two units.

Finishing

Refer to the **Basic Sewing Instructions** for some hints on squaring your top, attaching your borders, preparing your backing, sandwiching and quilting your quilt, and preparing and attaching the binding. Consult the **Cutting Instructions** above for the specifics in preparing your border strips.

Variations

Additional rows of "mountains" with more blocks per row could be added to enlarge the quilt. Additional yardage would be required. Consider making four separate **Catskill Mountainscape** quilts — one for each season, and hang them seasonally in your home.

If you would like to make **Catskill Mountainscape** in a different size, you might also consider using a different size strip for your **Design Blocks**. Refer to **Variations** in **Basic Sewing Instructions** to calculate the finished size of this quilt. Yardage requirements would have to be recalculated.

Detail of Catskill Mountainscape with home machine quilting

Heart's Delight

Over the last couple of years I've needed to make several baby quilts. This design was inspired by these babies. We want to let them know how much they are loved while making a baby quilt that will be used.

Highlights

Skill Level:	Confident Beginner
Strips:	**16** strips **1 ½" × WOF**
Design Units:	**28** — **12** dark-tipped and **16** light-tipped units
Background Units:	**28** half-square triangles
Background Squares:	**4** squares measuring **6" × 6"**
Background Rectangles:	**8** rectangles measuring **6" × 11 ½"**
Unfinished block size:	**6" × 6"**
Finished quilt size:	**37" × 48"**

Heart's Delight pieced by Lynn Lauzon-Russom and long-arm machine quilted by Eileen McCabe

Materials

Strips:	¼ yard each of a light, medium-light, medium-dark, and dark fabric **(S1-S4)** This pattern is fat quarter friendly
Background:	2 ½ yards
Border:	⅓ yard *or* use scraps left over from the **Design Blocks** (see photograph above)
Backing:	1 ½ yards — no cutting needed
Binding:	⅓ yard
Batting:	Throw size

Cutting Instructions

> **NOTE:** You will have at least **4** dark-tipped **Design Units** left over. You may use them to create a pillow sham, add them to your backing, or save them for another **Project**.

Fabric	Cut	Subcut	Additional Cuts
Strips	Cut 4 strips **1 ½" × WOF** from each fabric **S1-S4**	Sort into **4** sets arranged light to dark.	None
Background Units	3 strips **6 ½" × WOF**	Cut **14** squares **6 ½" × 6 ½"**	Cut each squares into **2** half-square triangles ◿ for a total of **28** half-square **Background Units**.
Background Rectangles	2 strips **12" × WOF**	*Vertically cut* **8** rectangles **11 ½" × 6"**. You will get **6** rectangles from one strip and **2** from the other.	**Note**: Cut these units vertically, not horizontally, for best economy of fabric.

Fabric	Cut	Subcut	Additional Cuts
Background Squares	Use the remainder of the 2nd strip from above	Cut **4** squares **6" × 6"**	None
Border	**4** strips **2 ½" × WOF** *or* **1** strip **2 ½" × WOF** from each fabric **S1-S4**	None	None

Assemble Heart's Delight in Rows as Follows

> **NOTE:** Follow the Basic Sewing Instructions for constructing your Design Blocks. Sliver trim blocks to a uniform square size. Pay attention to the orientation of the **Design Blocks** in each row.

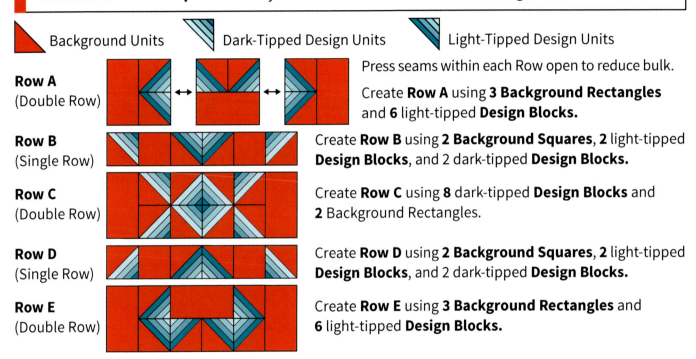

Background Units   Dark-Tipped Design Units   Light-Tipped Design Units

Row A (Double Row)

Row B (Single Row)

Row C (Double Row)

Row D (Single Row)

Row E (Double Row)

Press seams within each Row open to reduce bulk.

Create **Row A** using **3 Background Rectangles** and **6** light-tipped **Design Blocks.**

Create **Row B** using **2 Background Squares**, **2** light-tipped **Design Blocks**, and **2** dark-tipped **Design Blocks.**

Create **Row C** using **8** dark-tipped **Design Blocks** and **2** Background Rectangles.

Create **Row D** using **2 Background Squares**, **2** light-tipped **Design Blocks**, and **2** dark-tipped **Design Blocks.**

Create **Row E** using **3 Background Rectangles** and **6** light-tipped **Design Blocks.**

Carefully match and lock the seams as you sew your rows together. Join **Rows A & B**, then add **Row C**. Join **Rows D & E**, then add this unit to the **Rows A-C** unit. Press these seams open to reduce bulk.

Finishing

Refer to the **Basic Sewing Instructions** for help in squaring your top, attaching your borders, preparing your backing, sandwiching and quilting your quilt, and preparing and attaching the binding. Consult the **Cutting Instructions** above for the specifics in preparing your border strips.

Variations

If you would like to make **Heart's Delight** in a different size, you might consider using a different size strip for your **Design Blocks**. Refer to **Variations** in **Basic Sewing Instructions** to calculate the finished size of this quilt. Yardage requirements must be recalculated for any of these variations.

Detail of Heart's Delight pieced by Carolyn Dollard and mid-arm machine quilted by Kathryn Greenwold

Nautilus

This pattern explores the spiral, a design that occurs in nature and is a symbol used in many cultures: Native American, ancient Greek, Celtic, and Christian. It boasts of strong lines with minimal design elements and expanses of background space allowing for creative quilting.

Nautilus pieced and mid-arm machine quilted by Kathryn Greenwold

Highlights

Skill Level:	Confident Beginner
Strips:	**24** strips **2" × WOF** — **6** sets
Design Units:	**18** — all with dark tips
Background Units:	**18**
Background Squares:	**10** squares 8 ⅜" × 8 ⅜"
Background Rectangles:	**4** rectangles 8 ⅜" × 16 ¼"
Unfinished Block Size:	8 ⅜" × 8 ⅜"
Finished size with borders:	60" × 60"

Materials

Strips and Borders:	1 yard of fabric **S1** — **strip sets and inner border**
	¾ yard each of fabrics **S2 and S3**
	1 ½ yards of fabric **S4** — **strip sets and outer border**
Background:	2 yards
Backing:	4 yards
Binding:	½ yard – perhaps the same as **S4** (outer border fabric)
Batting:	Twin size

Cutting Instructions

Fabric	First Cut	Subcut	Subcut
Strips	6 strips **2" × WOF** each from fabrics **S1-S4** or select **24** strips from a **2 ½"** strip pack and cut them down to **2" × WOF**.	Sort into **6** sets of **4** strips each.	None
Background Units	3 strips **9 ¼" × 9 ¼"**. You only need to cut **1** square from the **3rd** strip.	Cut each strip into **4** squares **9 ¼" × 9 ¼"**. Set the remainder of the **3rd** strip aside for the next step.	Cut each square into **2** half-square triangles ◩ for a total of **18** for the **Design Blocks**.
Background Squares	2 strips **9" × WOF**, plus the remainder of the **3rd** strip from the **Background Units.**	Cut **10** squares 8 ⅜" × 8 ⅜".	None
Background Rectangles	2 strips **9" × WOF**	Cut **4** rectangles 8 ⅜" × 16 ¼"	None

Fabric	First Cut	Subcut	Subcut
Inner Border	**6** strips **2 ½" × WOF** from fabric **S1**	None — set aside	None
Outer Border	**6** strips **4 ½" × WOF** from fabric **S4**	None — set aside	None

> **NOTE:** All of the **Design Blocks** for **Nautilus** will have dark-tipped **Design Units**. Pay attention to the orientation of the **Design Blocks** in each row. You will have **18** light-tipped **Design Units** left over. Save them for another **Project** such as **Barn Raising** which uses only light-tipped **Design Blocks**.

Assemble Nautilus in Rows as Follows

 Background Units   Dark-Tipped Design Units

Follow the Basic Sewing Instructions for constructing your Design Blocks. Sliver trim the blocks to a uniform square size. You will need to make **6** strip sets, cutting **6** half-square triangles from each set.

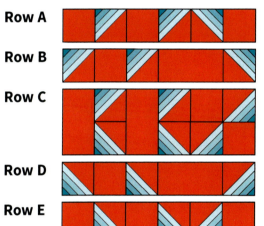

Row A

Row B

Row C

Row D

Row E

Press the seams in **Row A** to the right. Press the seams in **Row B** to the left. Continue to alternate the pressing of these seams to assist in matching and locking the seams when assembling rows.

This is a double row that must be assembled in units.

Rows D & E mirror **Rows A & B**. Assemble them carefully.

Sew **Rows A & B** together. Press all seams between Rows open to reduce bulk. Sew **Row C** in units. Then sew it to the **Row A/B unit**. Sew **Rows D & E** together. Add it to the **A/B/C unit**.

Finishing

Refer to the **Basic Sewing Instructions** for some hints on squaring your top, adding borders, preparing your backing, sandwiching and quilting your quilt, and preparing and attaching the binding. Consult the **Cutting Instructions** above for the specifics in preparing your border strips.

Butterfly Frenzy pieced by Mary Ellen Tardiff from the Nautilus pattern and long-arm machine quilted by Karen Gibbs

Variations

If you would like to make **Nautilus** in a different size, you might consider using a different size strip for your **Design Blocks**. Refer to **Variations** in **Basic Sewing Instructions** to calculate the finished size of this quilt. Yardage requirements must be recalculated for any of these variations. You might also make more blocks and/or add a border or two. Yardage requirements would need to be recalculated.

Crossroads

Crossroads creates an X-pattern meeting in the center with "paths" radiating outward. It is inspired by the images of broken arrow from Native American weavings and baskets, a symbol of peace.

Highlights

Skill Level:	Confident Beginner
Strips:	**2 ½"** strips — **6** sets:
	4 Design Units per strip
Background:	12 squares **12" × 12"** for
	24 half-square triangle
	Background Units
	12 squares **11 ½" × 11 ½"**
	6 rectangles **11 ½" × 22 ½"**
Unfinished Block Size:	**11 ½" × 11 ½"**
Top with Three Borders:	**84" × 102"**

Crossroads pieced by Lee Poremba and long-arm quilted by Kris Zimmer

Materials

Strips:	**1** strip pack — **24** strips 2 ½" × **WOF**
	or the equivalent of **24** strips 2 ½" × **WOF** from your stash
	or ½ yard of **4** fabrics **(S1–S4)** — light, medium light, medium dark, and dark
Background:	4 ¼ yards
First Border:	⅔ yard
Second Border:	½ yard — perhaps the same as your background fabric
Third Border:	2 yards
Backing:	3 yards of **108"** wide *or* 9 yards standard width fabric cut in **3** equal pieces
Binding:	¾ **yard** — See the **NOTE** below before purchasing additional fabric
Batting:	Queen size

> **NOTE:** If your background fabric is at least **42"** wide (after removing the selvages), you may be able to use the leftover backing fabric for your binding. See the **Background Cutting Guide** below.

Cutting Instructions

Fabric	Cut
Strips	Select **24** strips from a strip pack *or* cut **6** strips 2 ½" × **WOF** from each fabric **S1-S4**.
Background	Follow the **Background Cutting Guide** on the following page.

Fabric	Cut

Borders
     First Border
     Second Border
     Third Border
	9 strips **2 ½" × WOF**
	9 strips **1 ½" × WOF**
	5 strips **4 ½" × WOF** for the top and bottom outer borders
	6 strips **6 ½" × WOF** for the side outer borders

Backing	If using **108"** wide fabric no cutting is necessary If using standard width fabric, cut **3** equal pieces each measuring **108" × WOF**

Background Cutting Guide

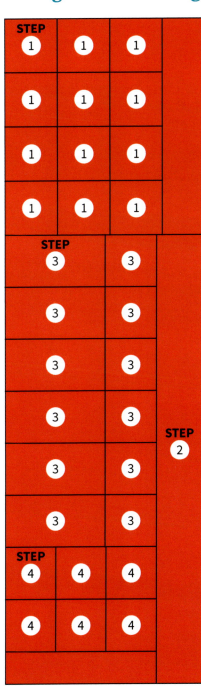

Step 1: Background Units

Cut 4 strips **12" × WOF**.

Trim the selvage and subcut each strip into **3** squares **12" × 12"** for a total of **12** squares.

Subcut each square into **2** half-square triangles to yield **24** triangles ◪ for the **Design Blocks**.

Step 2: Binding Strip

If your fabric is at least **42"** (after removing the selvages) you may choose to cut a **LOF** strip **34" × 105"** for the background cuts below. This will yield about **8"** from which to cut **4** strips **2" × 105"** for binding. Otherwise you will need ¾ yard additional fabric for the binding.

> **NOTE:** The squares cut in **STEP 1** are **12" x 12"**. In **STEPS 3 & 4** they are **11 ½" x 11 ½"**. Be vigilant in both cutting and placement of these units.

Step 3: Background Rectangles & Squares

Cut **6** strips — **11 ½" × WOF**

Trim selvages and subcut each strip into
    1 background rectangle **22 ½" × 11 ½"**
    1 background square **11 ½" × 11 ½"**
    for a total of **6** each.

Step 4: Remaining Background Squares

Cut **2** strips — **11 ½" × WOF**.

Trim selvages and subcut each strip into **3** squares **11 ½" × 11 ½"** for a total of **6** more background squares.

Assemble Crossroads in Rows as Follows

 Background Units Dark-Tipped Design Units Light-Tipped Design Units

> **NOTE:** Row D is a double-wide row.

Row A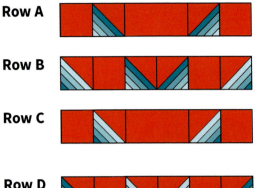

Row B

Row C

Row D

Row E

Row F

Row G

Assemble **Rows A & G** using **2** light-tipped **Design Blocks**. Throughout assembly, pay attention to the orientation of the blocks and placement of the light- and dark-tipped **Design Blocks**. Mark these **Rows A & G**.

Assemble **Rows B & F** using **2** dark-tipped and 2 light-tipped **Design Blocks**. Alternate the direction you press the seams between blocks for better matching of the blocks when sewing the rows together. Mark them.

Assemble **Rows C & E** using **2** dark-tipped **Design Blocks**. Press the seams between blocks in the same direction as for **Rows A & G**. Mark them.

Assemble the double **Design Block** units for **Row D** first, then construct this double row. You will use **4** light-tipped and **4** dark-tipped **Design Blocks**.

Assemble **Rows A/B/C**, paying attention to the orientation of the **Rows** as you sew them together.

Assemble **Rows E/F/G** in the same way. Add **Row D** to the **A/B/C unit**, then add the **E/F/G unit**. Press the seams between **Rows** open to reduce bulk.

Finishing

Refer to the **Basic Sewing Instructions** for some hints on squaring your top, adding the borders, preparing your backing, sandwiching and quilting your quilt, and preparing and attaching the binding. Consult the **Cutting Instructions** above for the specifics in preparing your border strips and binding. If you would rather not use this remaining background fabric for binding, cut **9** strips **2 ¼" × WOF** from the ¾ yard of fabric purchased to make a continuous binding.

Variations

If you would like to make **Crossroads** in a size larger or smaller than the ones included in this book, you might consider using a different size strip for your **Design Blocks**. Refer to **Variations** in **Basic Sewing Instructions** to calculate the finished size of this quilt. The borders for **Crossroads** should be proportional to the size of your blocks. Yardage requirements must be recalculated for any size variation.

Detail of Crossroads with long-arm quilting

Times Square

Times Square is the heart of New York City. I wanted to recreate the visual excitement of the neon lights which brighten the sky 24 hours a day.

Highlights

Skill Level:	Intermediate
Strips:	**24** strips **2 ½" × WOF** or equivalent yardage (fabrics **S1-S4**)
Design Units:	**24 — 12** light-tipped and **12** dark-tipped units
Background Units:	**24** half-square triangles
Background Squares:	**1** square **22 ½" × 22 ½"**; **8** squares **11 ½" × 11 ½"**
Background Rectangles:	**4** rectangles **11 ½" × 33 ½"**; **4** rectangles **11 ½" × 44 ½"**
Unfinished Block Size:	**11 ½" x 11 ½"**
Finished Quilt Size:	**88" × 88"**

Times Square pieced by Lynn Reynolds Makrin and long-arm custom quilted by Mandy Leins

Materials

> **NOTE:** The simplicity of design for this quilt lends itself to a novice as well as experienced quilter. Do not be limited by the colors used in the quilt pictured here. It could be equally dynamic with a light background and bright colors in the **Design Blocks**.

Strips:	**24** strips measuring **2 ½" × WOF** from a strip pack sorted into **6** sets *or* **½** yard each of 4 fabrics **S1-S4**
Background:	**6 ¼** yards
Binding:	Is included in the background fabric *or* **⅝** yard of another fabric
Backing:	**2 ¾** yards of a **108"-wide** or **8 ¼** yards of standard width fabric cut in **3** equal **2 ¾** yard (**99"**) pieces sewn together lengthwise
Batting:	Double size

Cutting Instructions

Fabric	Cut
Strips	Select **24** strips **2 ½" × WOF** *or* cut **6** strips **2 ½" × WOF** from 4 fabrics **S1-S4** Sort your strips into **6** sets of **4** strips each arranged from lightest to darkest.
Background	Follow the **Background Cutting Guide** on the following page.

Background Cutting Guide

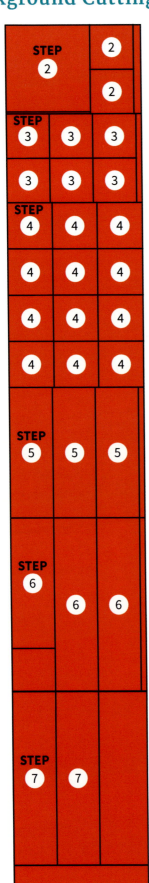

Step 1:
Cut (or tear) at **36"** along the **LOF**. Set aside the remaining **5-6"** to use for your binding.

Step 2:
Cut **23"** from the **36"** wide background fabric
Subcut into **1** square **22 ½" × 22 ½"** and **2** squares **11 ½" × 11 ½"**

Step 3:
Cut **23" × 36"** from the background
Subcut into **6** squares **11 ½" × 11 ½"**

> **NOTE:** The squares cut in **STEPS 2 and 3** are **11 ½" × 11 ½"**. In **STEP 4** they are **12" × 12"**. Be vigilant in both cutting and placement of these units.

Step 4:
Cut **48" × 36"** from the background
Subcut **12** squares that measure **12" × 12"**
Cut these squares into **24** half-square triangles for the **Design Blocks** ◩

Step 5:
Cut **34" × 36"** from the background fabric
Subcut **3** rectangles **11 ½" × 33 ½"**

Step 6:
Cut **45" × 36"** from the background fabric
Subcut **2** rectangles **11 ½" × 44 ½"** and **1** rectangle **11 ½" × 33 ½"**

Step 7:
From the remaining background fabric cut **2** rectangles **11 ½" × 44 ½"**

Follow the **Basic Sewing Instructions** for constructing your **Design Blocks**. Sliver trim the blocks to a uniform square size.

Assemble Times Square in Rows as Follows

 Background Units   Strip Pieced Design Units

> **NOTE:** Placement of dark- and light-tipped **Design Blocks** is not critical to this pattern. Place your blocks in an arrangement that is pleasing to you.

Press seams to the background fabric or open when constructing your Rows. Press the seams open when sewing your Rows together. Match and lock your seams as you put the rows together.

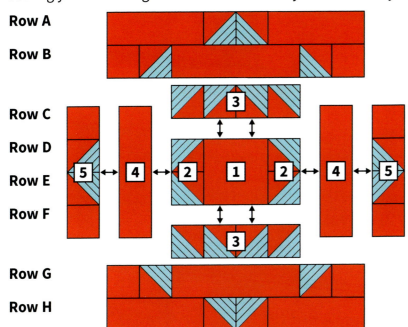

Row A
Row B
Row C
Row D
Row E
Row F
Row G
Row H

Construct **Rows A and B**. Sew **Row A** & **Row B** together.

Sew the center **Rows C, D, E, and F** as one unit beginning with the center square (**22 ½" x 22 ½"** - **#1** on this Chart).

Attach the side double **Design Block** units (**#2**), then the top and bottom **4 Design Block** units (**#3**). Add the left and right background units (**#4 – 11" x 44 ½"**), and then the left and right units with **2 Design Blocks** and **2** background squares each (**#5**).

Construct and sew **Rows G & H**. Sew **Rows G & H** together.

> **NOTE: Rows A & H** and **B & G** are the same, but are oriented differently. Pay attention as you assemble these Row sets and attached them to the center unit.

Finally, sew the **Row A/B** unit to the top of the **central unit (Rows C, D, E and F)** and add the **Row G/H** unit to the lower edge of your quilt top.

Finishing

Refer to the **Basic Sewing Instructions** for some hints on squaring your top, preparing your backing, sandwiching and quilting your quilt, and preparing and attaching the binding. Consult the **Cutting Instructions** above for the specifics in preparing your border strips.

Variations

If you would like to make **Times Square** in a different size, you might consider using a different size strip for your **Design Blocks**. Refer to **Variations** in **Basic Sewing Instructions** to calculate the finished size of this quilt using different size strips. Yardage requirements must be recalculated.

Detail of Flowers in Times Square with custom long-arm quilting

Italian Tile

I have always admired the inlaid tiles in the floors of old buildings and Italian palazzos. The geometry of these tiles lends itself beautifully to the geometry of quilting. This design is my attempt to translate these classic designs into one of my own creations.

Italian Tile pieced by Lynn Reynolds Makrin and long-arm machine quilted by Eileen McCabe

Highlights

Skill Level:	Intermediate
Strips:	**2" × WOF** strips — **9** strip sets
	If using a strip pack, choose **36** strips and cut them down to **2"** wide
Design Units:	**44** — **20** light-tipped and **24** dark-tipped half-square triangles
Background Units:	**44** half-square triangles of **Background A** (cream in the photograph above)
Background Squares:	**28** squares 8 ⅜" × 8 ⅜" — **Background A**
	12 squares 8 ⅜" × 8 ⅜" — **Background B** (taupe in the photograph above)
Background Rectangles:	**8** rectangles 8 ⅜" × 16 ¼" — **Background B**
Unfinished Block Size:	8 ⅜" × 8 ⅜"
Finished Quilt with Borders:	94" × 94"

Materials

Strips:	2 ¼ yard scrappy fabrics cut into strips **2" × WOF**
	or ⅝ yard each fabrics **S1-S4** (light, medium-light, medium-dark, dark)
	or 36 strips from a **2 ½"** strip pack, cut down to **2" × WOF**
Background A:	3 ¼ yards (cream in the photograph above)
Background B:	1 ¾ yards (taupe in the photograph above)
Inner Border:	¾ yard
Outer Border:	1 ¼ yard
Binding:	⅝ yard
Backing:	3 yards **108"** wide backing fabric
	or 9 yards standard width fabric in **3** equal lengths and sewn together lengthwise.
Batting:	King size

Cutting Instructions

Fabric	Cut	Subcut
Strips	9 strips **2" × WOF** from fabrics **S1-S4**	Sort into **9** sets of **4** fabrics each
Background A Squares	7 strips 8 ⅜" × WOF	28 squares 8 ⅜" × 8 ⅜". You will get **4** squares from each strip for a total of **28**

Fabric	Cut	Subcut
Background A **Background Units**	**6** strips **9 ¼" × WOF**	**22** squares **9 ¼" × 9 ¼"**. You will get **4** squares from each strip. Then cut **22** squares into **2** half-square triangles ◺◹ for the **Design Blocks**.
Background B **Squares**	**3** strips **8 ⅜" × WOF**	**12** squares **8 ⅜" × 8 ⅜"**. You will get **4** squares from each strip for a total of **12**.
Background B **Rectangles**	**2** strips **16 ½" × WOF**	Vertically cut **8** rectangles **8 ⅜" × 16 ¼"**. You will get **4** rectangles from each strip for a total of **8**.
Inner Border	**8** strips **1 ½" × WOF**	Set aside.
Outer Border	**9** strips **4 ½" × WOF**	Set aside.

Block Assembly

Follow the Basic Sewing Instructions for constructing your Design Blocks. Sliver trim your blocks to a uniform size. Create **9** strip sets using fabrics **S1-S4** or your strip pack sets. You will need **24** dark-tipped and **20** light-tipped **Design Units**. Begin cutting the strip sets with a dark-tipped unit.

Quilt Assembly

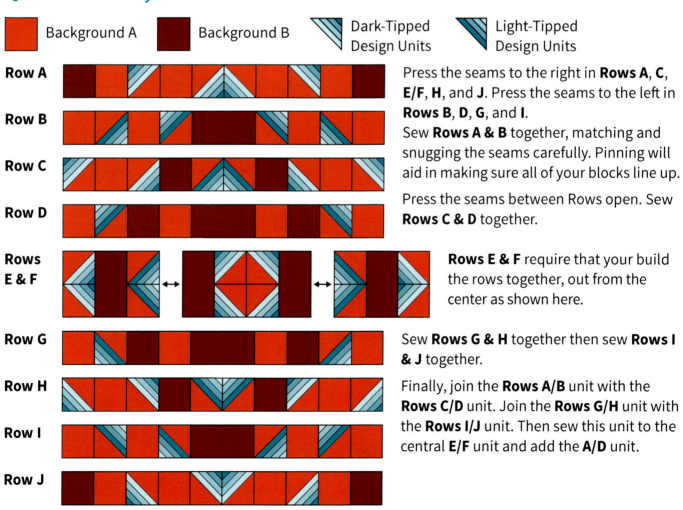

Press the seams to the right in **Rows A**, **C**, **E/F**, **H**, and **J**. Press the seams to the left in **Rows B**, **D**, **G**, and **I**.
Sew **Rows A & B** together, matching and snugging the seams carefully. Pinning will aid in making sure all of your blocks line up.

Press the seams between Rows open. Sew **Rows C & D** together.

Rows E & F require that your build the rows together, out from the center as shown here.

Sew **Rows G & H** together then sew **Rows I & J** together.

Finally, join the **Rows A/B** unit with the **Rows C/D** unit. Join the **Rows G/H** unit with the **Rows I/J** unit. Then sew this unit to the central **E/F** unit and add the **A/D** unit.

Finishing

Refer to the **Basic Sewing Instructions** for help in squaring your top, adding borders, preparing your backing, sandwiching and quilting your quilt, and preparing and attaching the binding.

Variations

If you would like to make **Italian Tile** in a different size, you might consider using a different size strip for your **Design Blocks**. Refer to **Variations** in **Basic Sewing Instructions** to calculate the size your quilt would be using a different strip size. Yardage requirements would have to be recalculated.

Detail of Italian Tile with long-arm machine quilting

Note the additional borders in this version of Italian Tile.

Italian Tile pieced by Deb Kriefels and long-arm machine quilted by Laurie Collins

Helpful Hints

▶ When planning a new quilt, measure the bed to determine the size of the quilt. There are many online resources available or seek help at your local quilt shop.

▶ If using fabrics from your stash for any quilt, take swatches with you when you go to purchase coordinating yardage. Don't assume you will remember the colors.

▶ Use a light weight thread for piecing or applique. This will give you flat, even seams. A neutral color that blends with all of your fabrics works best for piecing. Grey for cool colors and beige or tan for warm colors.

▶ Take pictures of your quilts. Make a label for the back with the name of the quilt, source of the pattern, date you finished it, and any other information you would like to record, especially if the quilt was a gift for someone. You will have a history of your quilting and be able to see how you have evolved as a quilter.

Foundations

The inspiration for Foundations came from a crumbling building foundation my family came upon while hiking in the Catskill Mountains of New York. We could still see where rooms had been, but most of the walls had fallen apart. This abstract design is based on what I sketched following that hike.

Foundations pieced by Lynn Reynolds Makrin and mid-arm machine quilted by Kathryn Rippeteau Greenwold

Highlights

Skill Level:	Intermediate/Advanced
Strips:	20 strips **1 ½" × WOF** (**5** sets of **4** fabrics — **S1-S4**)
Design Units:	**36** — **21** light-tipped and **15** dark-tipped
Background Units:	**36** — **18** squares **6 ½" × 6 ½"**
Background Squares:	**14** squares **6" × 6"**; **1** square **11 ½" × 11 ½"**
Background Rectangles:	**10** rectangles **6" × 11 ½"**; **2** — **6" × 17"**; **2** — **6" × 22 ½"**
Unfinished Block Size:	**6" × 6"**
Finished Quilt Size:	**48" × 55"**

Materials

Strips:	¼ yard each of 4 fabrics — **S1-S4**
Background:	2 ¼ yards
Binding:	½ yard *or* use what is left after trimming the backing once the quilting is done
Backing:	**3** yards
Batting:	Twin

Cutting Instructions

Fabric	Cut	Subcuts	Additional Cuts
Strips	5 strips **1 ½" × WOF** from each fabric S1-S4	None — sort into 5 sets	None
Background Units	3 strips **6 ½" × WOF**	6 squares **6 ½" × 6 ½"** from each strip — total **18** squares	Then cut each square into 2 half-square triangles ◩ for the **Design Blocks**
Background Squares and Rectangles	1 strip **12" × WOF**	1 square **11 ½" × 11 ½"** 1 rectangle **(cut vertically) 6" × 11 ½"** 2 strips **6" × remaining WOF**	None None 1 rectangle **6" × 22 ½"** from each of these strips — total **2**

Fabric	Cut	Subcuts	Additional Cuts
Background Rectangles	1 strip **6" × WOF**	2 rectangles **6" × 17"**	
Background Squares and Rectangles	2 strips **6" × WOF**	6 squares **6" × 6"** from each strip — total **12**	**None**
Background Squares and Rectangles	3 strips **6" × WOF**	3 rectangles **6" × 11 ½"** from each strip — total **9**	**1** square **6" × 6"** from the remainder of each strip — total **3**

Block Assembly

Follow the Basic Sewing Instructions for constructing your Design Blocks. Sliver trim the blocks to a uniform square size.

- **Strip Sets / Design Units:** Create 5 strip sets using fabrics S1-S4
Beginning with a light-tipped **Design Unit**, cut each strip set into **5** light-tipped and **4** dark-tipped design units for a total of **21** light-tipped **and 15** dark-tipped **Design Units**. You will only need to cut **1** light-tipped **Design Unit** from the **5th** set. Select **15** dark-tipped **Design Units** you want to use and set the rest aside for use in another **Project** (or on the back of your quilt).

- **Design Blocks:** Sew the **Design Units** to the **Background Units** — **21** light-tipped and **15** dark-tipped units.

Quilt Assembly

> **NOTE:** You will construct each row as shown below. Note that some rows are double and some are single. Pay attention to the orientation of each block as you assemble the rows. This is important for the execution of this abstract design.

 Background Units   Dark-Tipped Design Units   Light-Tipped Design Units

Row A (Double Row)

Use **3 Background Rectangles 6" × 11 ½"**, **6** light-tipped and **3** dark-tipped **Design Blocks**, and **3 Background Squares 6" × 6"**.

Row B (Double Row)

Use **1 Background Square 11 ½" × 11 ½"**, **1 Background Rectangle 6" × 11 ½"**, **4** dark-tipped and **4** light tipped **Design Blocks**, and **4 Background Squares 6" × 6"**.

Row C (Single Row)

Use **1 Background Rectangle 6" × 22 ½"**, **1** light-tipped and **1** dark-tipped **Design Block**, and **1 Design Rectangle 6" × 11 ½"**.

Row D (Double Row)

Use **4 Background Rectangles 6 × 11 ½"**,
5 light-tipped and **2** dark-tipped **Design Blocks**,
and **3 Background Squares 6" × 6"**.

Row E (Single Row)

Use **3 Background Squares 6" × 6"**, **3** dark-tipped
Design Blocks, and **1 Background Rectangle
6" × 17"**.

Row F (Double Row)

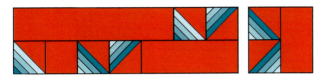

Use **1 Background Rectangle 6" × 22 ½"**,
2 dark-tipped and **5** light-tipped **Design Blocks**,
1 Background Rectangle 6" × 17", and
1 Background Unit 6" × 11 ½".

> **NOTE:** Press the seams between blocks to one side. Alternate the direction these seams are pressed to assist in matching and locking the seams between rows.

Sew Rows **A** through **C** together. Press the seams between Rows open to reduce bulk.

Sew Rows **D** through **F** together. Finally join these two larger units to complete your quilt top.

Finishing

Refer to the **Basic Sewing Instructions** for help in squaring your top, preparing your backing, sandwiching and quilting your quilt, and preparing and attaching the binding.

Variations

There are no borders in this version of **Foundations**. You might want to add a border or two. Additional yardage would be required.

If you would like to make **Foundations** larger or smaller, use a different size strip for your design blocks as shown in **Variations** in **Basic Sewing Instructions**. Yardage requirements would have to be recalculated.

Detail of Foundations with home machine quilting

Helpful Hint

▶ Use the following guidelines in choosing which needle to use in each situation.

Piecing cotton prints	Universal or Ball Point 80/12 or 90/14
Piecing batiks or heavier fabrics	Microtex size 80/12, 90/14 or 100/16 (for denim etc.)
Securing applique motifs by machine	Universal or Ball Point 70/11 or 80/12
Machine quilting	Microtex 80/12 or 90/14 on your home machine, 100/16 or 120/18 for long-arm quilting

Glossary

Background Unit The elements in the quilt top that are not made up of strip-pieced triangles. This will include the "solid" half-square triangles in your **Design Blocks** as well as supplemental units required for specific projects.

Design Block The pieced block you will work with in designing your quilt from this book. Each **Design Block** includes one strip-pieced half-square and one background half-square unit.

Design Units The half-square triangles cut from your strip-pieced sets to create half of your **Design Block**.

In-the-Ditch Quilting along seam lines either by hand or machine to stabilize areas of the quilt and give emphasis without obvious stitch lines showing on the surface.

Locking Seams If your seams have been pressed in opposite directions row to row they will "snug" together to create a perfect corner where the blocks meet. Use this technique to keep your rows straight and well pieced throughout construction of your **Project(s)**. It is a technique that can be used in creating many quilt patterns. Pin these joins and sew carefully for best results.

LOF Length of Fabric — used in yardage and Cutting Instructions.

Project One of the quilts in this book. There are 10 projects included along with instructions to create a Traditional Amish Shadows quilt.

Quilt-As-You-Go A quilt making technique where sections of the quilt are completed including quilting and then assembled into the larger whole. There are many books and online instructions available if you are interested in this technique.

Venus and Mars made and machine quilted by Lynn Reynolds Makrin

S1, S2, S3, & S4 Designations for your strip fabrics. S1 is light, S2 is medium-light, S3 is medium-dark, and S4 is dark.

Sliver Trim Trimming just a bit from the side of a block or pieced unit to straighten the edges and square the corners.

Spray Sizing This is not the same as spray starch. It adds body to your fabrics and is especially helpful when pressing long or bias seams. There are several commercial products available at most quilt shops. You can also find a recipe to make your own spray sizing online.

Strip Pack A standard strip pack is made up of 40 strips measuring 2 ½" × WOF. They are sold commercially under several different names. Occasionally a half-pack is offered which consists of 20 strips. They are available at your local quilt shop and online.

Strip-Piecing Sewing WOF (see below) strips together before cutting **Design Units**.

Value The lightness or darkness of a fabric *regardless of color*.

Value Viewer There are several commercial products available to use when looking at fabrics to determine their color value (the depth of coloration light to dark). However, red or green cellophane or photo cells can also be used. Use red with cool colors and green with warm. Looking through the colored strip removes the visual color of the fabrics you are looking at through the viewer, leaving only the value (light, medium, dark).

Wings The little points that stick out once the **Design Blocks** are assembled. They need to be trimmed to reduce bulk in the seams and to make piecing your blocks more accurate.

WOF Width of Fabric — used in yardage and Cutting Instructions.